Teaching for Recall &

Analysis

Improving Student Achievement in

World History

R. Michael Pryor

ISBN-10   0692367977

ISBN-13   978-0692367971

Pryolino Press

Chicago, Illinois 60614

Printed in the United States of America

For learning, love, and laughter.

Other works from the Teaching for Recall & Analysis series:

Teaching for Recall & Analysis: New Strategies for Improving Student Achievement in Social Studies

Teaching for Recall & Analysis: Advanced Floor Timelines for U.S. History

Teaching for Recall & Analysis: Interactive Venn Diagrams for U.S. History

Also by R. Michael Pryor

Alexander McGillivray and the Creek Confederacy: The Struggle for the Southern Backcountry

Essential American Principles: A User's Guide to American Political Documents

For additional information:

www.teachingforrecall.com

Table of Contents

How to use this book:

Improving Student Achievement in World History is part of the *Teaching for Recall & Analysis* series of books. This series provides educators with effective tools that will enable more students to experience success in academically challenging courses. These hands-on strategies help students develop the abilities that are needed in order to excel on the various "mastery of content" exams. Rigorous final exams are a central aspect of programs such as Advanced Placement and International Baccalaureate. If students are to experience success in these courses, they must recall and analyze a much greater amount of information than is required in a typical social studies class. This is a reality that many of the current "best practices" teaching methods fail to acknowledge!

These teaching strategies were designed for courses like college placement World History, which requires a student to comprehend, memorize, and later analyze a large amount of academic information. However, the flexible nature of these strategies would benefit students enrolled in numerous other courses. This teaching method is inexpensive and works well in a wide variety of academic settings. The strategies are easily integrated with existing educational practices and are purposely constructed in a way that ensures maximum instructional flexibility.

The goal is to help all students experience success when grappling with a curriculum that is heavily-laden with academic content. All of the books from the *Teaching for Recall & Analysis* series are designed for educators who want their students to possess the ability to analyze, recall, and then re-evaluate previously learned academic content; in order to create a better performance on AP, IB, SAT subject test as well as end-of-course assessments and state graduation exams. If students are shown how to analyze, organize, and recall information; they will never again have to say "I know the information, but I do not test well."

About the Author:

R. Michael Pryor is an educator and member of Achieve Learning Systems. A driving goal of Achieve Learning Systems is to provide the benefits of academic success and deeper intellectual analysis to a larger general population.

Teaching for Recall & Analysis

Improving Student Achievement in

World History

"Real knowledge is to know the extent of one's ignorance."

-    Confucius 551 - 479 BCE

Chapter One

Micro Assessments & Myelination

When students listen to a lecture, engage in an historical simulation, or create a multimedia project on a certain topic; how much of the information from these activities was actually absorbed by the students? In other words, just because students "worked" with the information does not mean that they "know" the information. A student can make a beautiful poster or brochure, but how much of the academic content from this assignment did this student actually learn? What information from this activity can students recall in a day, a week, or a month? If students cannot remember the classroom's academic material, and recall it when needed; they will struggle on any final "mastery of content" exam.

When one looks at fields outside of the classroom environment, a pronounced pattern emerges. Successful pilots, musicians, scientist, and athletes spend thousands of hours practicing, reflecting, and reviewing their respected fields of work. Highly skilled individuals do not analyze a situation, an arrangement, a procedure, or a technique only once. Pilots will spend innumerable hours reviewing potential situations that they may encounter in flight, while musicians repeat a musical arrangement until it is nearly perfect. A scientist will spend countless hours in the lab analyzing the results of an experiment; similar to how an athlete will devote an immense amount of time practicing in order to achieve a championship level performance. In the end, what all of these individuals are doing is performing a micro assessments every time they test their ability to accomplish a certain task. They are experiencing repeated exposure to the skill, ability, or information that they want to acquire and develop.

For most students, studying a topic once or twice is not enough exposure for the brain to analyze and memorize the specific academic content. This means that analyzing information, as well as later recalling this information; are skills that students must practice if they are to achieve this ability on their own. Working with interactive Venn diagrams will help students retain more information, which is especially important for any course that is judged by a standardized, content mastery, final exam. The Venn diagram strategy creates numerous micro assessment moments, which provides a quick fact check of the academic content that a student has learned. The principle of a micro assessment is critical for any class that possesses a challenging academic curriculum that is heavy on facts and details.

Repeated assessment of a student's level of knowledge is essential if one is to maximize learning. The traditional practice of using quizzes and test is an excellent tool for checking student learning. The uncertainty for an educator arises when a length of time has passed since the last quiz or test, leaving a teacher unsure as to whether students have mastered or even still remember a curriculum's facts and concepts. By using the principle of micro assessment, teachers can quickly check their student's level of knowledge, which allows them to distinguish between what students "think" they know, versus what they "actually" know.

The concept of using Venn diagrams is not new, and is in fact a well-established teaching tool in many academic disciplines. The interactive Venn diagram strategy is an updated version of a traditional Venn diagram, designed to meet the demands of an academically challenging curriculum. These approaches were initially created for Advanced Placement U.S. History classes which possessed an open enrollment policy, but they are readily adapted to many other academic disciplines.

Some educators may consider a micro assessment to be the same thing as a formative assessment, which is usually described as classroom practice with the curriculum's material. The opposite of formative assessments are summative assessments (standardized tests, end-of-unit exams, etc.), which are sometimes seen as being more of a legitimate accountability measurement. Micro assessments initially resemble formative assessments, but it moves far beyond the level of simple classroom practice.

Formative assessments are sometimes seen as "busy" work, with students acting in an automated, robot-like fashion as they complete assigned work in the classroom. However, micro assessments with strategies such as interactive Venn diagrams are not something that students can fake by just "going through the motions." Strategies with a micro assessment component have a correct answer and will reinforce previously taught concepts. With the micro assessment principle embedded in strategies such as the interactive Venn diagram, educators are able to spend less time giving assessments, but still have a measure as to whether their students are learning.

For any course with a challenging curriculum, there is a constant struggle between how many days of teaching are used for classroom instruction versus the number of days used for assessment. Educators must help their classes acquire all of the information in the curriculum, while simultaneously finding time to verify that the students are learning the specific details of the curriculum. To perform these vital pedagogical components takes time, something that is in short supply; hence micro assessments blend the elements of instruction with that of assessment.

Micro assessments and the process of myelination are essentially connected to each other, due to the fact that the act of engaging in a micro assessment encourages the physical process of myelination. At the most basic level, a person learns when the process of myelination occurs in the brain. Myelination is the thickening of the myelin layer that surrounds the electrical connections between the axons and the neurons in the brain. This myelin layer, or sheath, insulates nerve fiber and allow electric signals in the brain to travel at a much greater speed. In fact, a myelinated nerve fiber allows signals to travel 100 times faster than a non-myelinated fiber! This means that the more myelination that occurs in the brain, the faster it can process, analyze, and recall information.

These myelin sheaths in a student's brain are what teachers are trying to grow as they teach new academic material. At the most elementary level, when information is remembered by the brain and is retrievable at will; it has been myelinated. Repeated physical practice or exposure to stimuli is what thickens the brain's billions of myelin sheathed nerves. The process of myelination is stimulated by students practicing a new ability, which means that the myelinated fiber in student's brains becomes more pronounced each time they practice a new ability.

Visual Analogy of Myelination (the "lines" represent new information):

――― ― ― ― ―

1. This represents a person's initial exposure to new information. Some of the new information can be recalled, but part of the information is irretrievable because the brain has not developed sufficient neurological connections.

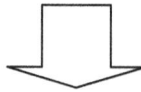

⬇

――――― ―― ―― ――

2. Additional exposure to the new information allows students to recall the information, but some gaps in knowledge still exist.

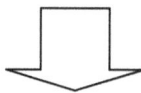

⬇

3. Information has been reinforced many times and can now quickly be recalled from memory. The act of recalling the information has actually thickened the myelin sheathed nerves cells.

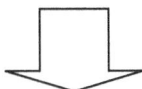

4. The information is now fully learned (retrievable at will) and incorporated with any existing information. However, if individuals do not continue to use and maintain this newly acquired myelinated section of nerve connections, the myelin sheath will weaken. This enhanced "information pathway" will slowly degrade if not routinely reinforced with use.

Imagine a person carrying goods down a rocky, dirt path. It is possible to move the goods down the path, but it is difficult and sometimes slow. Now imagine the same dirt path, but smoothed out and paved so that it is easier to travel on. Any variety of trade goods are now easily transferred down this paved walkway, but excessive goods can halt the flow of goods. Later, this walkway is turned into a single-lane road. The amount and ease of transportation has yet again expanded. Eventually, the transportation of materials is even more dramatically increased by widening this single-lane road into a multiple-lane super highway.

This simple analogy is similar to how the brain processes, stores, and retrieves information. Any information that students grapple with is similar to an "item" traveling down their brain's pathways, roads, and super highways. The more times students manipulate information, the more efficient the neurological pathways become in their brains. For teachers, a major educational goal is for their students to attain the ability to process and recall information much like goods traveling on a super highway. This means that lesson plans must be thoughtful and consistent in their approach. Otherwise, student learning stagnates, or they forget already learned (and myelinated) information because their previously formed synaptic pathways are not being challenged (used). Teachers should remember the following principles about the brain and learning:

❖ Students need repeated exposure to new information in order to produce the ability to reliably recall this information from memory.

❖ The more motivation that a student possesses to learn something, the less repetition is required to remember the new information.

❖ Less repetition of new information is required if students possess a personal connection to this new information.

The most current understanding of brain research supports strategies like the interactive Venn diagram activity that utilize learning principles such as information recall (myelination) as well as thoughtful reflection and reinforcement of previously-learned material (micro assessment). Engagement, analysis, and review are the key elements that will produce learning that is measurable and permanent.

Summary

- More permanent learning utilizes the action of myelination which will produce measurable results.

- Multiple repetition of information is needed in order produce an ability to recall that information.

- The continued use of micro-assessments encourages myelination.

- Academic information + practice at analysis & recall + myelination = measurable learning.

Chapter Two

The Essential Skills of Historical Analysis

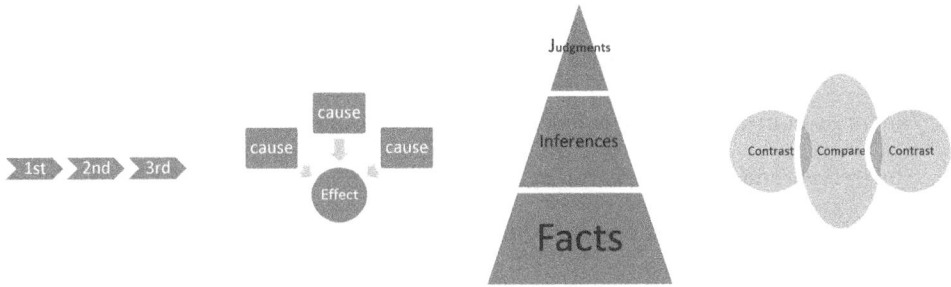

There are four critical skills that all students must possess in order to perform accurate historical interpretations and analysis. The application of these four skills provides students with a deeper understanding of historical eras, events, and sequence. The skills are as follows:

- **Chronological sequence (flow)**

- **Cause and Effect**

- **Facts, Inferences, and Judgments**

- **Comparing and Contrasting**

For proper historical analysis, students must possess the ability to apply these skills to any given time period or era. The interactive Venn diagram strategy is especially useful for comparing and contrasting various historical events and terms. When students practice this strategy they also develop an excellent foundation for the other historical skills. The analogy is similar to students exploring chemical compounds in a chemistry class. If students do not understand the basic structure of the periodic table, as well as the properties of the individual elements; they will have a far more difficult time understanding chemical compounds. The ability to analyze, create and compare inferences, as well as develop logical conclusions; all require a solid understanding of facts and details.

As students use the interactive Venn diagram strategy, they should remember the four historical skills as they compare and contrast the various pieces of academic information. Which topics in the timeline correlate to each other? Which terms are considered crucial turning points or watershed events? Do any patterns occur as individual events, people, and terms are compared and analyzed? Insightful inferences and thought-provoking evaluations do not occur unless an individual possesses a firm understanding of the details. Factual information is the foundation of sound historical analysis, which means that analysis without facts is just . . . opinion.[1]

"Creativity requires a mastery of what is known, including elements of discipline and synthesis – you can't think outside of the box if you don't have a box."

- Howard Gardner

---

[1] For a more detailed description of the essential historical skills, refer to *Teaching for Recall & Analysis: New Strategies for Improving Student Achievement in Social Studies*, 2nd ed., 2013.

Chapter Three

World History - Interactive Venn Diagrams

The Goal of Interactive Venn Diagrams:

Every teacher has encountered students who claim that they know the classroom material, but they do not test well. These students are often shocked to learn however, that even though they fully participated in all of the class activities and completed the homework assignments; they were unable to achieve an exemplary score on the final comprehensive course exam. For many of these students, the reason they are struggling on tests is not because of a lack of preparation; it is because they never learned how to fully "recall" previously analyzed information! This means that many students only possess a superficial grasp of the course's overall curriculum.

Teachers should reflect on what students have "really" learned at the end of every lesson plan. This is an important question to ask, especially if the students are judged by an end of the year, standardized, mastery of content exam (AP, IB, etc.). Advanced "college preparatory" classes require students to analyze and remember a much greater amount of academic content than is required in a typical class. If students are unable to remember previously reviewed material, then they possess little chance of properly analyzing and connecting it to newly learned information.

Analysis, reflection, and then a re-evaluating of an individual's original reflections take practice, effort, as well as time. Yet, the ability to analyze, recall, and then re-analyze the original information is a skill that is difficult to learn for many students. Practicing the ability to recall and analyze previously learned material is a specific skill that students need to possess if they are to succeed in academically challenging classes. It is essential that students possess the ability to analyze, remember, and then re-evaluate previously learned information.

One of the greatest challenges for a teacher is trying to convince students, parents, and sometimes other educators; that learning does not happen automatically. There is no guarantee that learning occurred just because a project was completed or a lengthy presentation was presented. If there was no thoughtful review or reflective practice over a period of time, with continued reinforcement; it is doubtful that any permanent learning transpired. Students may have demonstrated a working knowledge (very short term memory) of new academic information, but if there was no metacognition for future retrieval (myelination, compartmentalization, and memorization) of this new information; it is likely forgotten. Students will not be able to retrieve the information at will.

The Interactive Venn diagram strategy, as well as the other *Teaching for Recall & Analysis* strategies, will benefit educators who are searching for ways to help their students learn, organize, and recall more academic content. These strategies reinforce previously learned material while simultaneously introducing new information. The ability to mentally structure, and then recall, previously learned information provides students with the essential tools that will allow them to experience greater academic success. This is particularly true when teachers feels like they are racing the calendar and that there is not enough time in the school year to cover the entire curriculum. Coverage of a topic once or twice is not sufficient for the challenges presented to students by high stakes, content heavy examinations.

Venn diagrams are an excellent way to teach comparing and contrasting skills which are a critical piece of proper historical analysis. The strategy is named after the British logician and philosopher John Venn who first used the term Venn diagram in the late 19th century. Many educators are already familiar with the concept of a Venn diagrams and likely use them in their daily classrooms activities. Because Venn diagrams are an old teaching concept, many students are already familiar with this educational strategy. However, here is a brief description for those readers who have never used Venn diagrams or have forgotten about this instructional method. Once educators learn the fundamental principles behind this strategy, they can develop numerous variations based on the concept.

What are Venn Diagrams:

This is an excellent method for introducing and building upon critical thinking and inference skills. Venn diagrams, at the most basic level, are a collection of circles drawn together on the same horizontal plane. The purpose of the diagram is to show a logical relationship between two or more possible topics. In a Venn diagram, the grouping of common traits or features within a given circle means that these items have a logical connection to each other. The next image displays the basic principle behind a Venn diagram, with the left circle representing one topic (A) while the right circle represents another topic (B). The space in the middle, where the two circles overlap, represents information that both topics have in common.

The logic of a Venn diagram

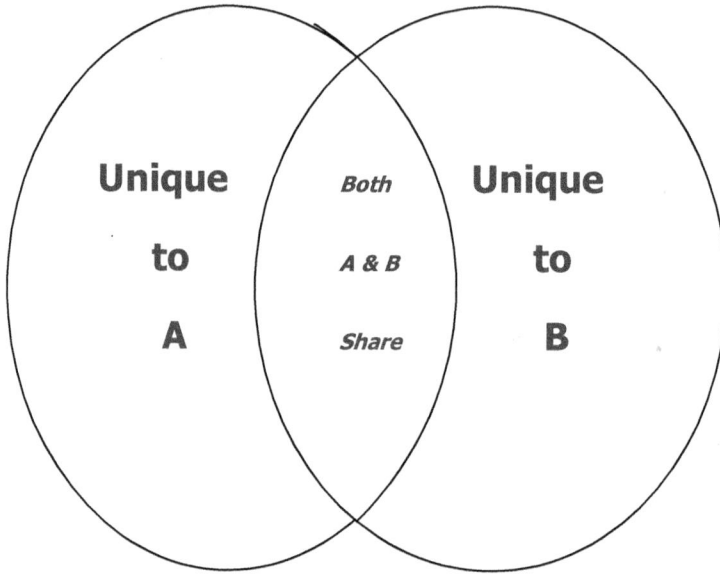

The image above displays an empty Venn diagram that compares two different items, in this case topic A and topic B. The part of the diagram where the circles merge represents information that is unique to both item A and item B. This section of diagram displays features that both "sides" share in common.

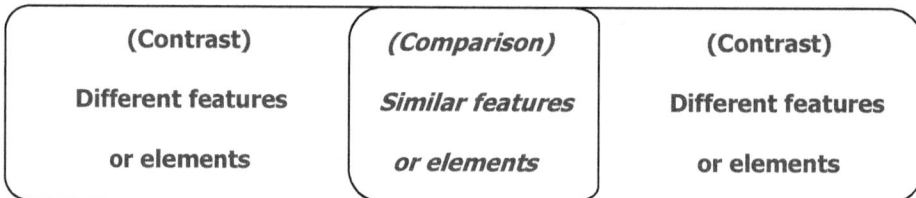

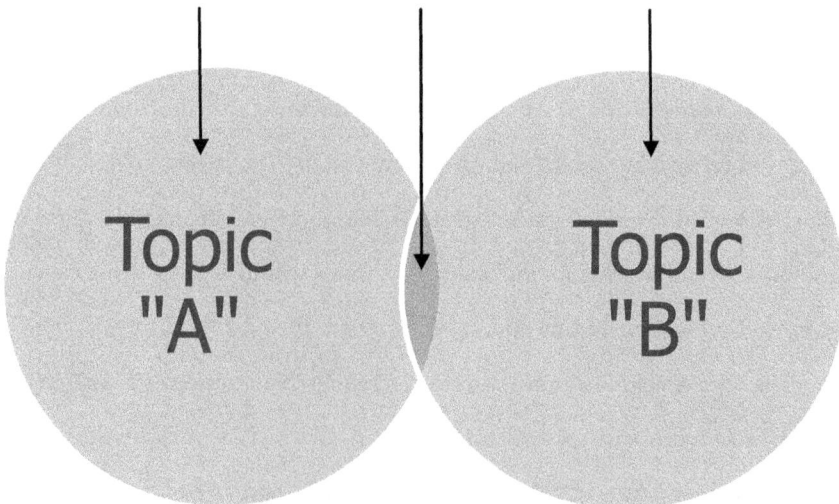

The topics or items that are comparable in a Venn diagram are too numerous to count, with a two topic Venn diagrams easily able to compare and contrast social movements, economic developments, or political figures. For example, during the 12th to 15th centuries, both the Inca and Mexica civilizations were prominent in the Americas. The Inca first settled in the Andean highlands near present-day Lake Titicaca and would later build a capital city named Cuzco. Spanning from north to south, their empire stretched over four thousand miles and was connected by a complex road system. In comparison, the Mexica (Aztecs) had migrated to present-day central Mexico and replaced the declining Toltec society. By 1345, they had built their capital city, Tenochtitlan and utilized a productive style of agriculture known as *chinampas*. In this example, the Venn diagram's left "circle" would list information about the Incan Empire, while the right "circle" would displays information that was unique to the Mexica.

The "common elements" that the Inca and Mexica societies both shared are displayed where the two circles of the Venn diagram overlap. In this example, both societies relied heavily on agriculture and practiced human sacrifices during religious ceremonies. Their respective religions were polytheistic and focused on worshipping the sun. Both empires declined with the arrival of Europeans and were conquered by conquistadors, later becoming part of the Spanish Empire. There are many other similarities between these two civilizations, with the task of finding their common elements becomes easier as a student's base of knowledge about these two subjects expands.

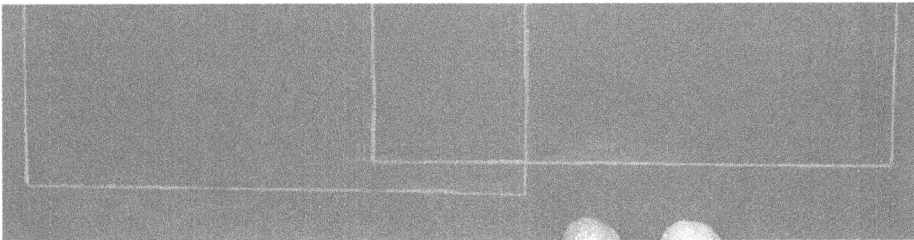

Inca

* Capital City - Cuzco
* Extensive North & South road system

Mexica (Aztecs)

*Capital City - Tenochtitlan
* Developed *chinampas* style of agriculture

"Common Elements"

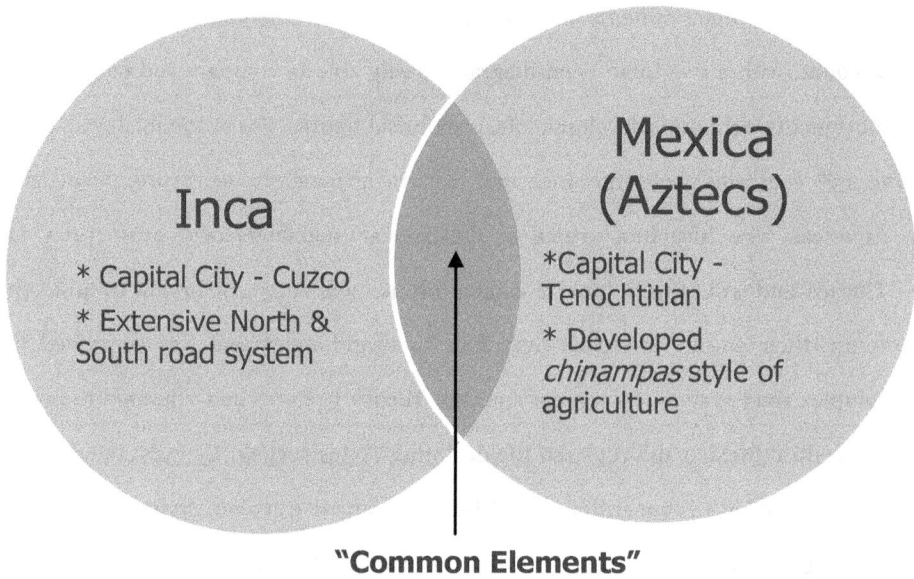

Once a class understands the basic principles of a Venn diagram, and understands the logic of the teaching strategy; an instructor can stop placing the information inside the Venn diagram's circles. Eventually, a teacher can simply draw the circles on the board, verbally state what terms are being compared and contrasted; and then proceed with the rest of the Venn diagram activity. When a class is able to utilize the Venn diagram at this level, writing the answers on the board will actually slow down the learning activity and disengage the students.

Furthermore, in the "common elements" section of a typical Venn diagram, there is usually not enough space available to list a significant number of items. Once students are familiar with the rhythm of activity, the act of writing terms into the Venn diagram circles is not required. Ultimately, a major goal of this activity is to create a sense of energy and enthusiasm for the curriculum's topics. The interactive Venn diagram strategy accomplishes this by creating a "game-like" atmosphere, but without sacrificing the integrity of learning activity. In other words, the teaching strategy possesses a game-like playfulness, but it is not a game. Student engagement is not the objective, the final goal is for students to develop and retain knowledge.

Venn diagrams are a useful teaching strategy, but there is a drawback in the way this activity is traditionally applied in the classroom. In general, as a teaching activity, this traditional strategy is fairly teacher-centered in its classroom application. Problems occur due to the fact that some students may have a difficult time staying focused on the information being presented and placed into the Venn diagram by the teacher. Any diagram placed on a board or projector screen is still basically a lecture format, with students becoming passive receivers of the information. This instructional approach is not inherently wrong, and there are times when direct instruction is necessary in order to clearly explain a difficult problem or a complex event. However, the lecture is sometimes over used in academically advanced classes, which means that students sometimes "tune out" and become disengaged from the classroom environment. A key goal of the interactive Venn diagram strategy is to move the focus of the information closer to the students.

How an Interactive Venn Diagram Works:

Here is a short explanation of the activity. In order to illustrate this point, the next Venn diagram will reexamine facts about the Paleolithic and Neolithic Eras.

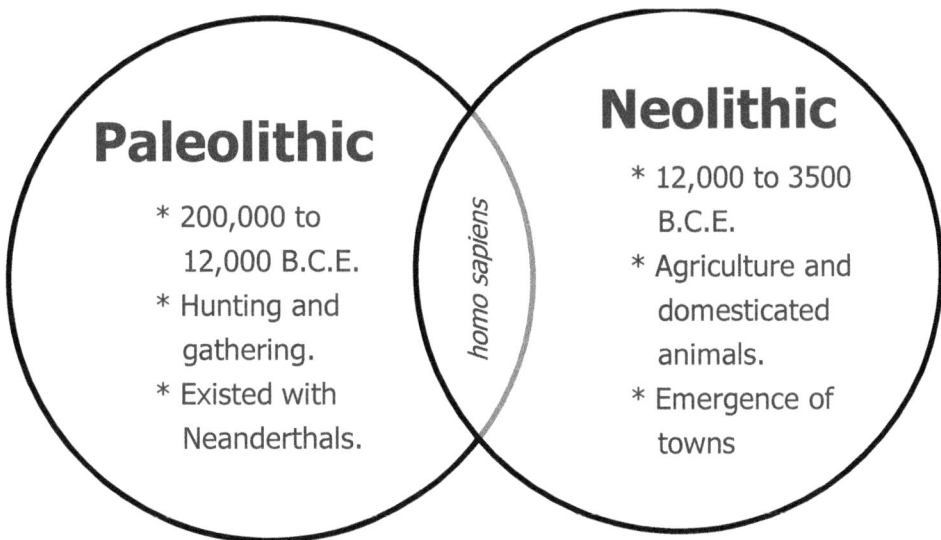

Paleolithic

* 200,000 to 12,000 B.C.E.
* Hunting and gathering.
* Existed with Neanderthals.

homo sapiens

Neolithic

* 12,000 to 3500 B.C.E.
* Agriculture and domesticated animals.
* Emergence of towns

1. A large Venn diagram in two colors is drawn on the chalk or whiteboard. For example, one Venn circle could be drawn in red while the other circle is drawn in black.

2. On the board, inside the red Venn circle, write the term *Paleolithic*; while inside the green Venn circle write the word *Neolithic*. Briefly inform the students that they will have to catch either a red or black ball, and then state an important fact about the topics written inside the circles on the board; however they must answer the Venn diagram that matches the color of the ball. In this case, the historical topics which are being compared are *Paleolithic* (red) and *Neolithic* (black). For example, if they catch a red ball, they must state a relevant fact about the *Paleolithic* Era. Explain to the students that after they have presented correct and relevant facts about their Venn circle topic, they should politely toss the ball to somebody else in the classroom who has not yet answered a question. The individual who catches the ball now also has to cite a correct and relevant fact about the *Paleolithic* or *Neolithic* Era.

3. The teacher initiates the activity by gently throw the balls to separate students in the classroom. Again, the balls should match the colors of the Venn diagram on the chalk or whiteboard, so in this example one ball was red while the other was black. However, if the Venn diagram on the board is composed of yellow and blue Venn diagram circles, then the Venn balls should also be yellow and blue in color.

4. As each student catches a ball, they must state historically relevant information about their topic. If a student catches the red ball, he or she has to present factual analysis about the topic written in the Venn diagram's red

circle (*Paleolithic* Era). Some possible examples are: Neanderthals existed alongside homo sapiens, created cave paintings, lived in small bands of about thirty to fifty people, etc.

5. After successfully presenting relevant facts, the teacher should ask students to list characteristics that both historical eras had in common (had developed trade networks, possessed complex languages, etc.).

The interactive Venn diagram strategy moves quickly, so even students with shorter attention spans can stay focused. A teacher is also able to utilize the principle of micro assessment, and check the level of student understanding as the class participates in the activity. By throwing the ball to each student in the classroom, and then following each "catch" with a question, in a few minutes a teacher quickly finds out what a class actually knows about a certain topic or even range of subject matter. This "catch and answer" effect encourages students to discover, confront, and remedy what they "actually" know, versus what they "think" know.

Pre-Venn Activities: Answer Ball

The answer ball strategy is an excellent activity for preparing students for the spontaneous nature of an interactive Venn diagram, while also allowing them to feel comfortable with the physical movement of the "Venn" balls. The activity incorporates the principles of movement and academic review into a classroom's learning environment. This strategy is a great warm-up activity for students and quickly develops their ability to think on their feet, while simultaneously checking their capacity to recall previously learned information.

How to use the answer ball strategy:

1. A teacher takes a "ball" from the Interactive Venn diagram strategy.
2. The teacher should lightly throw the ball to a student in the class.

3. When the student catches the ball, the instructor should then ask a previously studied academic content question.

4. The student should answer the question as quickly as possible.

5. Once students have answered the question, they should lightly throw the ball back to the teacher.

6. The instructor picks a new student and repeats the activity.

Initially, the answer ball activity may surprise some students and make them feel unprepared. However, when students catch the ball and then have to answer a question, the teacher is performing a quick micro assessment of learning. If students are unable to answer a teachers inquires, it soon becomes apparent that they do not know a sufficient amount of information about a given topic. In order to encourage participation, a teacher can assign points to students who were able to respond correctly during the activity. Understandably, some students may struggle when forced to answer a question simply due to stress of being "put on the spot" by the teacher. This little bit of extra stress is actually beneficial for student learning.

Recreating Test Anxiety: "Catch and Answer"

The circulation of the "Venn" balls around the classroom will create an elevated level of anticipation which simulates a feeling of test anxiety among students. Catching and answering questions in this manner gives students practice at not "freezing up" during a situation where their knowledge is tested. This may sound trivial, but during a high-stakes testing situation, much like a playoff game; students may freeze up and mentally "go blank" during an important exam. If students are unable to correctly answer questions during this activity, then they may struggle on a high-stake (high stress) exam.

A goal of many teaching strategies is for students to actively engage in the instructional activity, while being able to correctly recall and analyze previously learned knowledge. The addition of a ball toss component in a Venn diagram strategy allows the activity to generate classroom excitement and engagement. The catching of the ball and being placed on the "spot" forces students to test their ability to retrieve academic information. If students are unable to recall previously learned information – they have not really learned that information!

The straightforward nature of this activity provides students an opportunity to model and reflect on logical thinking and reviewing. Students will soon realize that simple pieces of information, when studied and compared to each other; create more complex pieces of information. Similar to building a jigsaw puzzle, when the individual pieces are compared to each other it appears simple, but as the sheer volume of pieces compared increases and the groups of attached pieces grow; a new and more complex pattern emerges. When students study on their own, they should model this thinking and reviewing process. As simple pieces of information combine to create a more complex narrative, this provides the foundation for deeper analytical exploration. When students can consistently recall basic pieces of information, they soon develop the awareness to see the "connections" between the facts, which gives them the ability to generate more complicated inferences and evaluations.

Using Venn Diagrams:

The next few images display the many different ways to construct a Venn diagram, which reinforces the fact that these diagrams are extremely flexible in their application. The features and relationships of the topics being compared will dictate the style and shape of the Venn diagram. There really is no one "best" diagram, only numerous options; however a two-topic Venn diagram is the simplest to use and easiest for students to understand. Creativity and variety will encourage learning and remind students to view the connections between information in as many different ways as possible.

The goal of the interactive Venn diagram strategy is to actively engage students while encouraging analytic reasoning and information recall. Teachers should explain to the students that the colored ball actually represent the individual circles of a Venn diagram. The use of different colored chalks or markers, along with matching colored balls; physically models the thought process that is required for comparing and contrasting academic information. The strategy utilizes the movement of these balls in order to produce a sense of motion and create an interactive learning experience. As simple as it sounds, motion in a classroom fires more of the brain's neurons, making students less likely to not pay attention.

Again, as the next picture demonstrates, the ball on the left (pink) corresponds to the part of the Venn diagram drawn with pink chalk, while the ball on the right (blue) connects to the portion of the Venn diagram drawn in blue chalk. If a teacher is using a white board, then have the ball's color match the color of the white board markers. Keep in mind that any color may be used for this strategy, just so the Venn diagram is easily visible for all of the students in the room. The colors of the ball or type of board (interactive whiteboard v. dry erase whiteboard v. chalkboard) are minor features. The goal is to extend the logic of the activity out into the classroom, and create a level of student engagement that is rigorous and content-based.

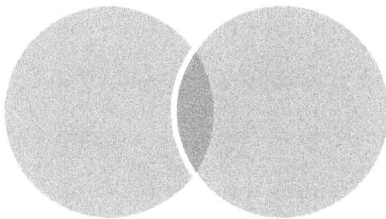

Venn diagram   v.   "interactive" Venn diagram

How to Make Interactive Venn Diagram Balls:

1. Select colored paper that closely matches the chalk or dry erase marker in the classroom. Next, take old newspapers or similar disposable paper and crimple it into a ball. Keep layering the paper around the paper wad until it is about the size of a grapefruit.

2. For the final outside layer, crimple the selected colored paper around the paper wad. When you are finished with this step, none of the newspaper layers should be showing.

3. Wrap the grapefruit-sized paper wad with transparent tape. Cardboard box sealant tape works well for this task. When finished, the colored Venn diagram balls should resemble the ones in the picture below.

If the Venn diagram circles on the white or chalk board are blue and pink diagram, then the accompanying blue and pink balls should be used in order to symbolically project the diagram out among the students. Using colored balls to physically extend a Venn diagram out into a classroom engages more students and encourages participation. The ultimate goal of the strategy is to have all of the students in a classroom actively engaging and analyzing academic information.

Initially, a teacher should quickly write down the student responses inside the appropriate Venn diagram's circle. Eventually, after students become familiar with this strategy, a teacher can skip writing the classroom's responses on the board. Using the Venn diagram in this manner allows a teacher to quickly evaluate previously learned material and judge how well students have learned previous objectives from the curriculum. The strategy becomes even more efficient if an educator already knows the answers to the Venn's comparisons. If a teacher has to pause to look up the answers – it breaks the lesson's flow and energy. Without any excessive pauses in the activity, in about five or ten minutes a teacher can quickly discern whether a class knows the subject matter. In addition, this act of "micro assessing" reinforces a central principle of a micro assessment by providing the class with an additional review of the information. This quick check of a student's previous "learning" will actually reinforce the same previously "learned" material!

Modifications for Students with Special Needs:

However, teachers should be aware of students with special needs. If the act of throwing balls in the classroom creates potential problems – simply change the act. Instead of throwing a ball to facilitate questioning, pull the student's name from a hat. This is accomplished by having all of the students in your class place their name on a slip of paper or an index card. When a teacher is leading the class through an interactive Venn diagram strategy, simply pull the student's name from a hat, bag, or box. The act of pulling a student's name out of a hat will replace the "ball toss" aspect of the interactive Venn diagram. Instead of students being selected by the act of catching a ball, they are now selected when their name is pulled from the hat. By not using the "Venn" balls some of the energy may dissipate from the activity, but now all students can easily participate in the lesson plan.

In addition, if any students are color blind, this issue is easily remedied by using colors that are visible for these students. Individuals with color blindness often have difficulty distinguishing between dark or light greens, reds, and browns. If this the case, simply pick a color for the Venn diagram balls that all students can easily recognize such as yellow and blue or black and white.

Three-Topic Venn Diagrams:

The same instructional approach that is used for a two-topic interactive Venn diagram is also utilized for a three-topic Venn diagrams, but the overall activity is more challenging for an instructor. When a three-topic Venn diagram strategy is done correctly, the classroom is like an orchestra with the teacher becoming a maestro. However, if the teacher has not sufficiently practiced using the two-topic strategy, then there is a risk that the classroom will literally turn into an out of control three-ring-circus; with the teacher becoming a struggling ringmaster. Educators should practice with the two topic diagram before attempting the three-topic version.

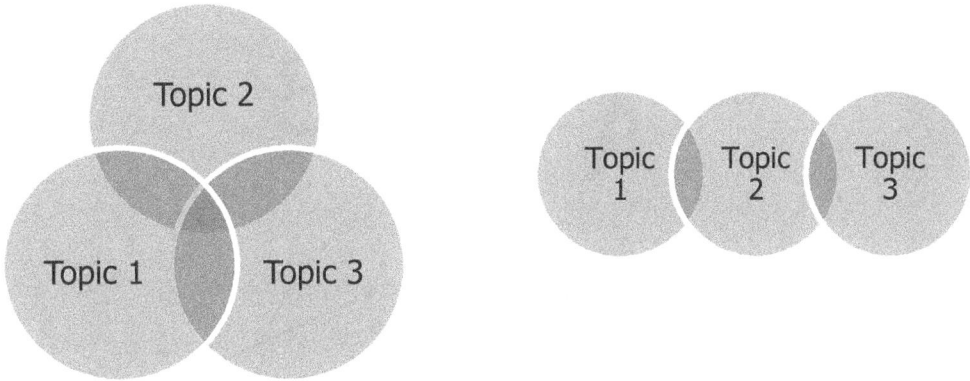

Three-topic Venn diagrams

In the three-topic diagrams shown on the previous page, the example on the left is useful when comparing and contrasting topics that all share a similar trait, but may not exist in chronological order. The example on the right is valuable for comparing and contrasting topics that possess a direct cause and effect relationship or chronological order. The image below illustrates a three-topic Venn diagram and explains the logic behind the activity. In this example, three separate topics (A, B, and C) are being compared and contrasted.

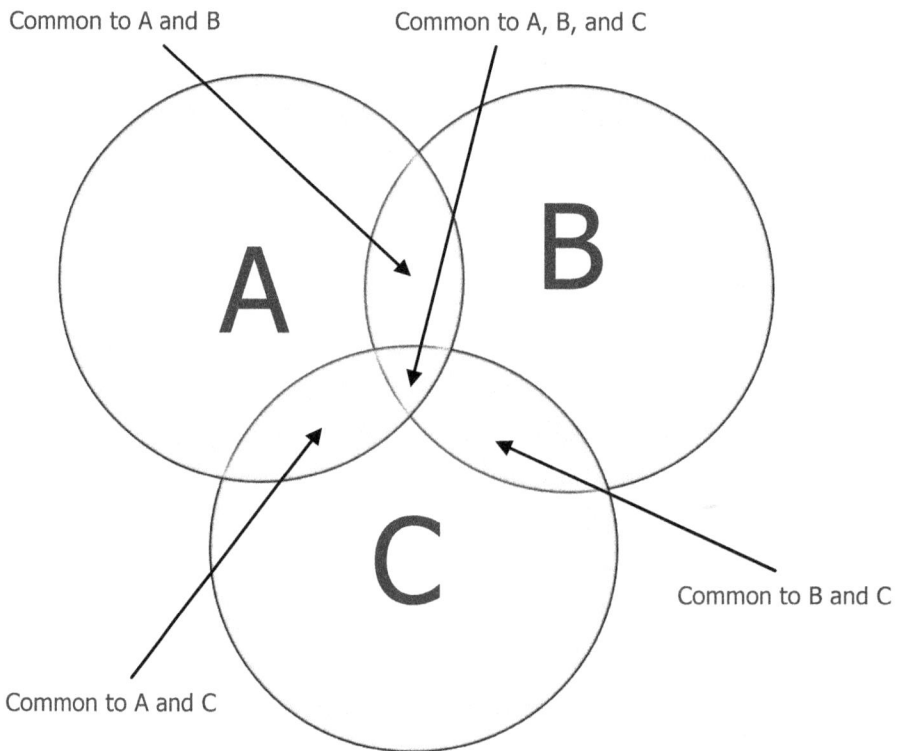

The logic of a three-topic Venn diagram

As was the case with the two-topic version, the teacher should have a Venn "ball" which corresponds to each circle of the Venn diagram. This means that educators will need three different colored Venn balls, which match the circles in three-topic Venn diagram; in order to conduct the activity. While the two-topic version engages two students simultaneously, the three-topic version has three students participating in the answering of questions. In classroom application the three-topic interactive Venn diagram moves and looks like a two-topic Venn diagram.

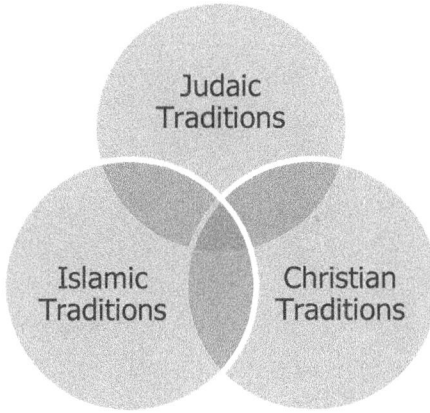

Three-topic interactive Venn diagrams

In the previous images, the picture on the right displays a Venn diagram with the diagram "circles" replaced with different geometric shapes (triangle and squares). How the Venn diagram "circles" are drawn is an individual style choice for a teacher, just so students can clearly differentiate between the topics being compared in the activity. However, irregular Venn circles are more difficult for a teacher to write information inside of due to the odd shapes.

As an instrument for review, when this strategy is done well, it is a beautiful thing to behold. The class and the teacher become fully engaged with the topic at hand, with all eyes and attention focused on the moving balls and the classroom analysis. Again, as a reminder, the educator needs to have a firm understanding of the topics being compared in order for this strategy to flow smoothly. If a teacher stops during the activity to look up answers to questions – the activity's energy will quickly dissipate. One goal of this strategy is to keep students engaged in the activity and not allow them to hide in their seats. Instructors must possess a thorough knowledge of the Venn diagram topics being compared in order to keep "things" moving.

Three-topic Venn diagram variations: 1 to 2 Venn diagram comparison

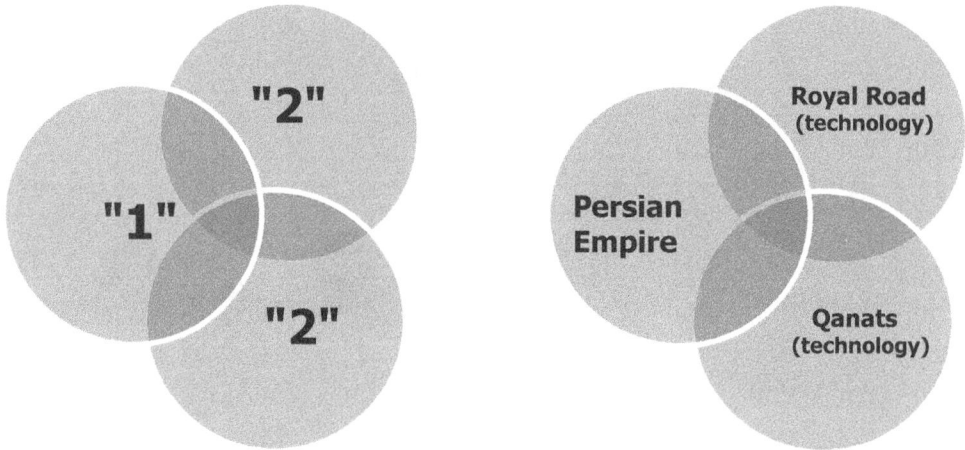

This is a more complex version of a three-topic Venn diagram which is useful when there are three items for comparison, but two of the items possess more in common than the third item. Three-topic Venn diagrams are great for showing an increased similarity between two items, yet still display the overall commonalities that exist between all three topics. The following are a few examples of possible 1 to 2 Venn diagram topics:

- The European powers that were the most successful at colonizing/invading the North American continent: the "1" could represent 17th century England which was a Protestant-dominated country. While the "2"s could represent 17th century Spain and France which were Catholic-dominated countries.

- Early United States political factions and leaders: the "1" could represent John Adams as a Federalist, while the "2"s could represent the Democrat-Republican ideals. One "2" is Thomas Jefferson (Democrat-Republican) while the other "2" would represent James Madison (Democrat-Republican).

- The diagram could explore the political factions that existed during the American Civil War such as the Republicans (1), Southern Democrats (2), and Northern Democrats (2).

The next diagram incorporates the principle of "chronological flow" or sequence of events for the post-classical era in China. Many sequenced events tend to have pattern that displays a *cause* and *effect* relationship, but this is not always the case. Whether two topics possess a true *cause* and *effect* relationship can actual develop into a classroom debate which encourages students to infer other pieces of information in order to prove or disprove any perceived historic relationships.

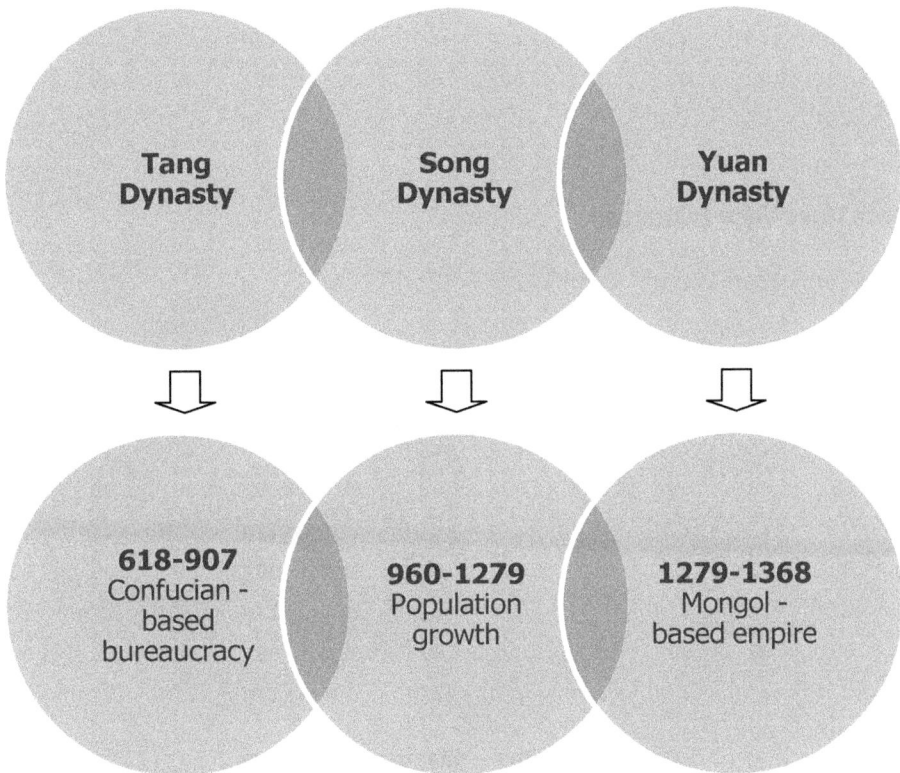

These previous two Venn diagrams, displayed above, are useful for showing sequence and change over time. In these diagrams, students could analyze why there was a transition from the Tang Dynasty to Song Dynasty, which was eventually followed by the Yuan Dynasty. The second three-topic Venn diagram displays the dates of the dynasty's existence as well as a major historical feature of that civilization; all of which correspond to the information in the series of dynasties in the first Venn diagram. There are numerous variations of the three-topic Venn diagram, with a teacher having almost limitless choices. Educators may choose to call their 1 to 2 Venn diagram a "2 to 3" diagram or an "A to the double B" diagram; all that is required is a little forethought and creativity.

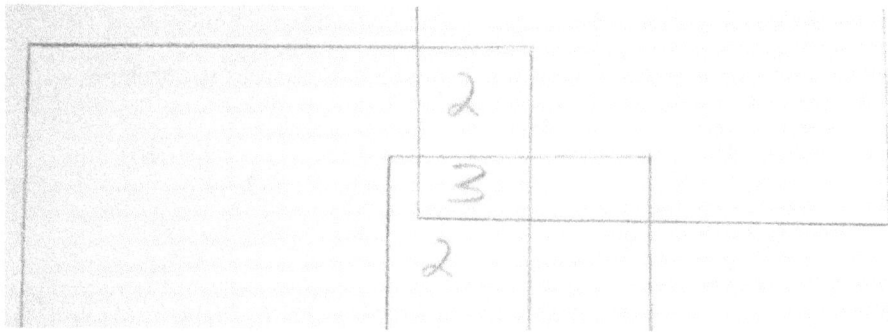

Four Topic Venn Diagams:

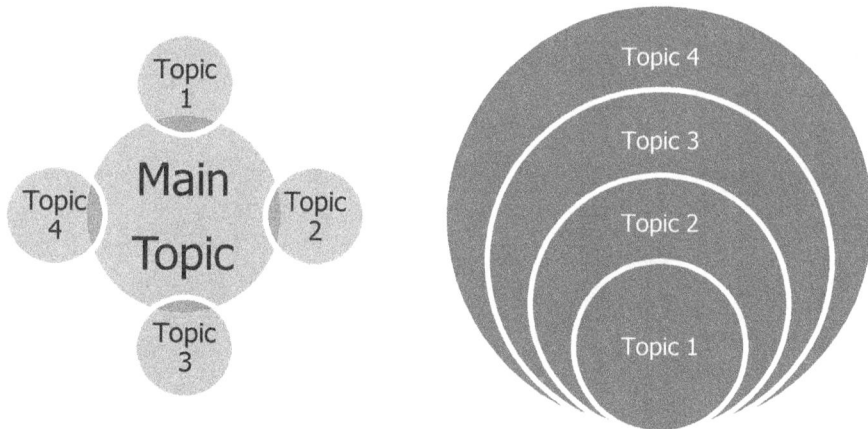

Venn diagrams – different variations

A two-subject Venn diagram is one of the easiest ways to compare and contrast topics, but with practice one can start using three or four topics during an activity. However, three or four topic Venn diagrams require more focus from both the instructor and the students. Teachers should experiment and discover what works best for their student's individual needs.

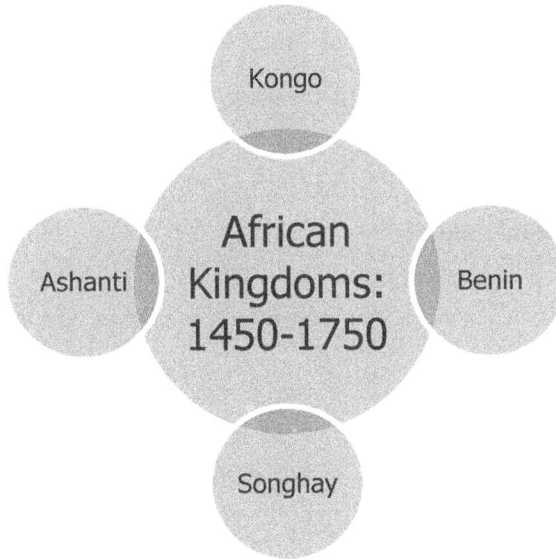

Humor is Essential:

Teachers must remember that academic rigor does not automatically equal boring. A teacher with a good since of humor can quickly ease classroom tension and allow students to feel less anxious. Less anxious students will inspire more classroom interaction while simultaneously creating a more relaxed class atmosphere. When both of these components are in place, it is much easier for an educator to have a positive impact on learning. However, students should not be so relaxed that they become disengaged from the classroom activities.

When most people reflect back on their favorite teachers, these educators were probably well-liked because of their sense of humor. Psychological studies reinforce this point by stating that humor enhances a classroom's academic performance, with students seeming to retain more information through the use of humor. In addition, these studies found that courses that possess a teacher with a sense of humor tend to receive better student reviews and have increased participation. A teacher's sense of humor can act like a social lubricant, which helps to facilitate classroom interactions. This means that if an educator is teaching a course that has a tremendous amount of academic content and is considered challenging, humor is a teacher's best friend. The challenge for a teacher is too make sure that the classroom humor maintains a focus that is academic in nature and reinforces the days learning objective.

Games and Academic Rigor:

Social studies classes are sometimes notorious for using "game-like" activities or simulations to engage and/or reinforce a learning objective. These simulations range from mock jury trials, event reenactments, to World War recreations. The goal is to make the lesson material seem more real and "pull" the students into the activity. If done properly, a class simulation can make a topic more real for students and hopefully create a more lasting impression. However, if simulations are designed and implement poorly, students see the activity as a waste of time and the entire class period is considered a "blow-off" day.

The principle philosophy behind using classroom simulations is well-intentioned, and can encourage as well as maintain student engagement during a learning activity. However, by the time a student reaches the high school level, finding "learning" games that are academic rigorous, and do not consume an excessive amount of time, is especially challenging. Game-like activities can engage students and create more excitement in the classroom, but problems arise as the complexity and amount of information in the curriculum increases. Which means as the academic material becomes more complex, the classroom simulations and games do not reflect this increased level of complexity and depth. Many classroom learning games overly focus on socializing, or on knowledge that is superficial and easily answered. Academic simulations that involve a great deal of higher-order thinking, along with the recall and analysis of previously learned material; are rare if non-existent. Furthermore, learning games/simulations that focus on more complex, higher-order thinking skills take a larger amount of instructional time to initiate, implement, and assess.

Learning is not always game; it takes effort, dedication, and time. Teachers can use humor to relax the students and create a "game-like" atmosphere, but they must constantly focus on academic relevance and rigor. Providing student with what they "need" versus what they "want" is a delicate balance for teachers. This means that there is often a struggle between what students "want" to do versus what they "need" to do. Students may enjoy playing games in the classroom, but this does not mean that these activities are the best use of instructional time.

Reviewing: Quick and Spontaneous

Learning sometimes looks a little messy, but this is not to be confused with disorganization. Teachers need to "jump around" in their curriculum in order to continually activate (check) pre-knowledge. References to current topics are crucial in order for students to make connections to prior events. Learning takes place when an individual makes connections from what they know, to what they did not know. However, the traditional approach to learning history often advocates focusing on one time period or topic, and not moving on until all students have mastered this specific time period or concept. The mastery of previously learned subject matter is essential if students are going to learn new subject material. New concepts are learned by the brain in a scaffolding-like manner, with newly acquired information attached to pre-existing information. However, as new content is learned, it is ideally attached to this older information. In order to ensure that previously learned knowledge is not forgotten, frequently review is necessary; this is the only way to ensure that students will retained the material that was covered a week, a month, or last semester.

The use of interactive Venn diagrams are an excellent method for quickly reviewing previous information, since the strategy is easy to implement, moves quickly, and engages students. However, interactive Venn diagrams are not meant to replace all other teaching strategies, they were simply created to augment the instructional environment and exist as one more tool in an educator's toolbox. As a point of caution, interactive Venn diagram strategies are not the same as a "drill and kill" approach to learning! If any strategy or activity is overused, it will become boring and non-beneficial to the students.

Summary

- Interactive Venn diagrams create engagement by having students catch balls and answer questions while analyzing a teacher-directed comparison.

- The motion of the Venn diagram balls, combined with student responses, is more engaging then a traditional Venn diagram teaching strategy.

- The interactive Venn diagram is an excellent review activity as well as a way to sharpen comparing and contrasting skills.

- There are numerous variations of the traditional Venn diagram such as 2 subject Venn diagrams, 1 to 2 Venn diagrams, as well as 3 and 4 topic Venn diagrams.

- This strategy reinforces the principle of micro assessments and the action of brain myelination.

"Anticipate the difficult by managing the easy."

-        Lao Tzu 604 ? – 531 BCE ?

Chapter Four

World History - Venn Diagram Topics

The following sample list of historical topics has been provided in order to assist with the implementation of the interactive Venn diagram teaching strategy. The lists of historical comparisons are far from complete and once educators are familiar with the activity they should create their own historical comparisons. The following list of Venn diagram topics is in chronological order and includes a wide variety of terms and concepts from world history. This list of topics is intended to provide an educator with a wide variety of historical events, individuals, and themes that work well for a Venn diagram compare and contrast activity.

The list of Venn diagram topics mentioned in chapter five exactly matches the list topics presented in chapter four. However, in chapter five the topics have been placed in pre-formatted Venn diagram charts. This provides educators with the opportunity to create an "answer key" that fits the individual needs of their students. As a reminder, an educational goal of this activity is to keep the "flow" of the Interactive Venn diagram activity moving, since a major objective of the strategy is to create a sense of energy and spontaneity in the classroom. If an educator does not know the answer to a student response, and then has to look it up; the effectiveness of the overall activity is diminished. The provided list of historical comparisons is far from exhaustive and educators are encouraged to modify it as needed. At the end of the day, it is not what the teacher knows -- but what the students can remember and explain.

Pre-Classical & Classical Era:
8000 B.C.E. to 600 C.E.

Early Societies & Civilizations

Paleolithic   v.   Neolithic

Neolithic Gender Relations

Female   v.   Male

Sources of Change

Diffusion   v   Independent Invention

Early Societies

Foraging   v.   Pastoral

Impact of Agriculture

Population   v.   Environment

Impact of Agricultural Revolution

Social Classes   v.   Economic

Stages of Metal Use

Copper (& Bronze)   v.   Iron

Early Civilizations

Mesopotamia   .v   Egypt

Early Civilizations

Indus Valley (Harrapan)   .v   Yellow River (Shang)

Early Civilizations

Mesoamerica   .v   Andean

Political Developments

Classical China   v.   Classical India

Political Developments

Classical Mediterranean   v.   Mesoamerica

Classical Civilizations

Trade Patterns   v.   Technologies

Political Structure of Classical China

Emperor   v.   Bureaucracy

Classical Civilizations

Social Structures   v.   Gender Structures

Major Belief Systems

Hinduism   v.   Buddhism

Major Belief Systems

Judaism   v.   Christianity

Major Belief Systems

Confucianism   v.   Daoism

Role of Women

Confucianism   v.   Hinduism

Role of Women

Buddhism   v.   Christianity

Classical Greece

Philosophy   v.   Science

Nature of Social Hierarchy

Confucianism   v.   Hinduism

Movements of Peoples

Germanic   v.   Bantu

Movements of Peoples

Hun   v.   Polynesians

Interregional "Networks"

Trade Routes   v.   Spread of Religions

Social Systems

Slavery   v.   Caste System

Empire Collapse (Decline)

Roman Empire (Western Europe)   v.   Han (China)

Post-Classical Era: 600 to 1450

New Civilizations & Empires

Africa   v.   Eurasia

Dar al-Islam

Economic Impact   v.   Cultural Impact

Islamic Influences

Arts   v.   Sciences

Dynasties -- East Asia

Sui   v.   Tang

Dynasties -- East Asia

Song   v.   Yuan

Mesoamerica

Aztec   v.   Inca

Asia

Mongol   v.   Delhi Sultanate

Europe

Byzantium   v.   Russia

Interregional Trade Networks

Indian Ocean   v.   Trans-Saharan

Interregional Trade Networks

Swahili Coast   v.   Silk Road

Economic Innovations

Tang   v.   Song

Contacts between Major Religions

Christianity & Islam   v.   Islam & Buddhism

Missionary Religious Efforts

Islam   v.   Buddhism

Cultural Patterns

Japan   v.   Vietnam

Chinese Influences

Korea   v.   Japan

Confucianism

Korea   v.   China

The Americas

Maya   v.   Inca

Europe

Feudalism   v.   Cities

Christianity (Division)

Roman Catholic   v.   Eastern Orthodox

Sudanic Empires

Songhay   v.   Mali

South/Southeast Asia

Delhi Sultanate   v.   Vietnam

Impact of Migrations

Afro-European   v.   Americas

Impact of Plague Pandemics

Societal Consequences   v.   Economic Consequences

Growth of Cities

China   v.   Americas

Sources of Change

Nomadic Migrations   v.   Urban Growth

Roles for Elite Women

Constraints   v.   Opportunities

Dar al-Islam

Unified Political/Cultural Entity   v.   Divided Political/Cultural Entity

Feudalism

Japanese   v.   European

Development of Political/Social Institutions

Western Europe   v.   Eastern Europe

Islamic Contacts

Sub-Saharan African   v.   European

Political Entities

Arab Caliphate   v.   Mamluks

European Feudalism

Serfs   v.   Lords

Impact of the Crusades

Economic   v.   Cultural

Impact of Viking Explorations

Economic   v.   Cultural

Impact of Mongol Expansion

Economic   v.   Cultural

Neo-Confucianism

Inside of China   v.   Outside of China

Indian Ocean Trading Patterns

Hindu-Buddhist Period   v.   Muslim Period

The Papacy

East–West Schism (1054)   v.   Western Schism (1378–1417)

Pre-Modern Era: 1450 to 1750

The Columbian Exchange

New World   v.   Old World

Technological Changes

Shipbuilding   v.   Navigational devices

Major Empires

Ottoman   v.   China

Major Empires

Mughal   v.   Tokugawa

Major Empires

Portugal   v.   Britain

Major Empires

France   v.   Russia

Major Empires

Aztec   v.   Spain

African Kingdoms

Kongo   v.   Oyo

African Kingdoms

Benin   v.   Dahomey

African Kingdoms

Ashanti   v.   Songhay

Role of Women

In Households   v.   In Politics

Slavery and the Slave Trade

Europe   v.   Africa

Population Trends

North and South America   v.   Europe and Africa

New Religions

Protestantism   v.   Vodun

New Religions

Sikhism v.   Zen

Intellectual Developments

Scientific Revolution   v.   Enlightenment

Developments in the Arts

Mughal v.   Europe

Developments in the Arts

East Asia   v.   the Americas

Rising European Dominance

Environmental Reasons   v.   Technological Reasons

Colonial Administrations

British   v.   Spanish

Coercive Labor Systems

Indentured Service   v.   Slavery

Development of Empires

Asia   v.   Africa

Development of Empires

Americas   v.   Europe

Imperial Systems

European Seaborne Empires   v.   Asian Land-based Empires

Russia's Interactions with:

China   v.   Ottoman Empire

Russia's Interactions with:

Western Europe   v.   Eastern Europe

Economic Exchange Systems

Andean   v.   Mesoamerican

Extent of Ottoman Expansion

Africa & Europe   v.   Asia

Slave Plantation Systems

Old World   v.   New World

Harems

Ottoman   v.   Chinese

Trade Relationships

Kongo   v.   Portugal

Foreign Policy (Relations)

Japan   v.   Mughal

Foreign Policy (Relations)

European   v.   Ottoman

European Exploration

Economic Reasons   v.   Social/Cultural Reasons

European Absolutism

Political Consequences   v.   Social Consequences

Protestant Reformation

Political Consequences   v.   Social Consequences

Rise of the Modern Era: 1750 to 1914

Global Changes in:

Technology   v.   Commerce

Global Changes in:

Communications   v.   Trade Patterns

Global Changes in:

Demographic   v.   Environmental

Global Changes in:

Medicines   v.   Migration Patterns

Industrial Revolution

Europe   v.   Americas

Industrial Revolution

Transformative Effects   v.   Differential timing in opposing societies

Industrial Revolution

Social Impacts   v.   Environmental Impacts

Emancipation

Slaves   v.   Serfs

Societal Changes

Social Structures   v.   Gender Roles/Structures

Political Movements & Independence Movements

United States   v.   Latin America

Revolutions

France   v.   China

Democracy Movements

Advances   v.   Limitations

Rise of Western Dominance (Imperialism)

Military Aspects   v.   Economic Aspects

Rise of Western Dominance (Imperialism)

Cultural Aspects   v.   Political Aspects

Rise of Western Dominance (Imperialism)

Colonialism   v.   Neocolonialism

Rise of Western Dominance (Imperialism)

Dissent & Reform   v.   Resistance & Rebellion

European Art

African Influences   v.   Asian Influences

Japan

Tokugawa   v.   Meiji

Serf/Slave Emancipation

Causes   v.   Effects

The Role of Women

Industrialized Regions   v.   Non-Industrialized Regions

Technological Innovation

European/British   v.   Asia/China

Latin American Independence Movements

Causes   v.   Effects

Early Phase of the Industrial Revolution

Japan   v.   Western European

Revolutions

French   v.   American

Revolutions

Haitian   v.   Mexican

Economic Systems & Theories

Capitalism   v.   Marxism

Intellectual Developments

Darwinism   v.   Social Darwinism

Reactions to Foreign Influence

Ottoman Empire v.   China

Reactions to Foreign Influence

India   v.   Japan

Rise of Nationalism

Japan   v.   China

Rise of Nationalism

Italy   v.   Egypt

Rise of Nationalism

France   v.   Germany

Rise of Nationalism

Pan Africanism   v.   Indian Congress Movement

Forms of Western Intervention

East Asia   v.   Southeast Asia

Forms of Western Intervention

Latin America   v.   Africa

Conditions of Elite Women (before 1850)

Latin America   v.   Western Europe

Women's Emancipation Movements

Europe   v.   North America

Trade Networks

Suez Canal   v.   Panama Canal

Contemporary Era: 1914 to Present

The World Wars

World War I　　v.　　World War II

New Patterns of Nationalism

Fascism　　v.　　Decolonization

Challenges to Democracy (Interwar Years)

Italy　　v.　　Germany

Authoritarian Regimes (Interwar Years)

South America　　v.　　Asia

War and Peace

The Holocaust　　v.　　The Cold War

Global Political Structures

League of Nations　　v.　　United Nations

Global Economic Structures

Developed Nations　　v.　　Developing Nations

Decline of European Influence

United States　　v.　　Asian Nations

War and Peace

Nuclear Weaponry   v.   International Organizations

The Great Depression

The Americas   v.   Europe

Social & Political Extremes

Racism (Apartheid)   v.   Genocide

Global Economic Developments

Pacific Rim   v.   Multinational Corporations

Social Changes

Changes in Gender Roles   v.   Changes in Family Structures

Social Revolution

Peasant Revolutions   v.   International Marxism

Social Reform

New Feminism   v.   Religious Fundamentalism

Spread of Marxism/Communism

Russia   v.   China

Soviet Union

Establishment   v.   Disintegration

Post-Colonial Africa

Political Conflicts   v.   Environmental Issues

Global Cultures

Science   v.   Consumer Culture

Patterns of Resistance (Religious Responses)

South Asia   v.   North America

Demographic Changes

Birth & Death Rates   v.   Urban to Rural Shifts

Environmental Changes

Deforestation   v.   Green/Environmental Movements

Diverse Interpretations

Cultural Diversity   v.   Cultural Convergence

Frames of Reference

The West   v.   The Developing World

Patterns of Decolonization

Africa   v.   South Asia (India)

Effects on the Roles of Women

Iranian Revolution   v.   Russian Revolution

Effects on the Roles of Women

Cuban Revolution   v.   Chinese Revolution

Effects of the World Wars

In Africa   v.   In Asia

Legacies of Colonialism

Middle East   v.   Latin America

Legacies of Colonialism

Africa   v.   Asia

Global Interactions

Sports   v.   Arts

Effects of Western Consumer Society

Social/Cultural   v.   Economic/Trade

Major Forms of 20th Century Warfare

The Great War   v.   World War II

Major Forms of 20th Century Warfare

Terrorism   v.   Guerilla

Cold War

Warsaw Pact   v.   NATO

Effects of Global Wars

Economics   v.   Political

Economic Growth in Asia

Japan   v.   "The Little Tigers"

Chapter Five

World History - Venn Diagram Topic Charts

The following charts match the list of Venn diagram topics that were presented in chronological order in chapter six. Empty space has been provided so that a teacher can add the necessary contrast and comparison answers. The overall goal of this strategy is to provide educators with quick reference points, so that they can maintain the "flow" of the activity. This Venn diagram strategy should move at a quick and energetic pace, while creating a slight level of test anxiety. As students become more familiar with the overall strategy, they will develop the capacity to leap from topic to topic and create new connections, inferences, and evaluations.

Example of possible teacher-generated contrast & comparison answers:

Dynasties -- East Asia

(Different)	(Similar)	(Different)
Song		**Yuan**
• 960-1279 • Rulers mistrusted military leaders • Economically prosperous and urban • Emergence of a market economy with paper money and credit	• Chinese empires during the high and late Middle Ages • Increase of foreign administrators into China • New technological developments	• 1279-1368 • Kublai Khan extends Mongol rule over East Asia • Unsuccessful invasion attempts of Southeast Asia and Japan • Weakened by bubonic plague and inflation

Pre-Classical & Classical Era: 8000 B.C.E. to 600C.E.

Early Societies & Civilizations

(Different) Paleolithic	(Similar)	(Different) Neolithic

Neolithic Gender Relations

(Different) Male	(Similar)	(Different) Female

Sources of Change

(Different) Diffusion	(Similar)	(Different) Independent Invention

Early Societies

(Different) Foraging	(Similar)	(Different) Pastoral

Impact of Agriculture

(Different) Population	(Similar)	(Different) Environment

Impact of Agricultural Revolution

(Different) Social Classes	(Similar)	(Different) Economic

Stages of Metal Use

(Different) Copper (& Bronze)	(Similar)	(Different) Iron

Early Civilizations

(Different) Mesopotamia	(Similar)	(Different) Egypt

Early Civilizations

(Different) Indus Valley (Harrapan)	(Similar)	(Different) Yellow River (Shang)

Early Civilizations

(Different) Mesoamerica	(Similar)	(Different) Andean

Political Developments

(Different) Classical China	(Similar)	(Different) Classical India

Political Developments

(Different) Classical Mediterranean	(Similar)	(Different) Mesoamerica

Classical Civilizations

(Different) Trade Patterns	(Similar)	(Different) Technologies

Political Structure of Classical China

(Different) Emperor	(Similar)	(Different) Bureaucracy

Classical Civilizations

(Different) Social Structures	(Similar)	(Different) Gender Structures

Major Belief Systems

(Different) Hinduism	(Similar)	(Different) Buddhism

Major Belief Systems

(Different) Judaism	(Similar)	(Different) Christianity

Major Belief Systems

(Different) Confucianism	(Similar)	(Different) Daoism

Role of Women

(Different) Confucianism	(Similar)	(Different) Hinduism

Role of Women

(Different) Buddhism	(Similar)	(Different) Christianity

Classical Greece

(Different)	(Similar)	(Different)
Philosophy		Science

Nature of Social Hierarchy

(Different)	(Similar)	(Different)
Confucianism		Hinduism

Movements of Peoples

(Different)	(Similar)	(Different)
Germanic		Bantu

Movements of Peoples

(Different)	(Similar)	(Different)
Hun		Polynesians

Interregional "Networks"

(Different) Trade Routes	(Similar)	(Different) Spread of Religions

Social Systems

(Different) Slavery	(Similar)	(Different) Caste System

Empire Collapse (Decline)

(Different) Roman Empire (Western Europe)	(Similar)	(Different) Han (China)

Post-Classical Era: 600 to 1450

New Civilizations & Empires

(Different) Africa	(Similar)	(Different) Eurasia

Dar al-Islam

(Different) Economic Impact	(Similar)	(Different) Cultural Impact

Islamic Influences

(Different) Arts	(Similar)	(Different) Sciences

Dynasties -- East Asia

(Different) Sui	(Similar)	(Different) Tang

Dynasties -- East Asia

(Different) Song	(Similar)	(Different) Yuan

Mesoamerica

(Different) Aztec	(Similar)	(Different) Inca

Asia

(Different) Mongol	(Similar)	(Different) Delhi Sultanate

Europe

(Different)	(Similar)	(Different)
Byzantium		**Russia**

Interregional Trade Networks

(Different)	(Similar)	(Different)
Indian Ocean		**Trans-Saharan**

Interregional Trade Networks

(Different)	(Similar)	(Different)
Swahili Coast		**Silk Road**

Economic Innovations

(Different)	(Similar)	(Different)
Tang		**Song**

Contacts between Major Religions

(Different) Christianity & Islam	(Similar)	(Different) Islam & Buddhism

Missionary Religious Efforts

(Different) Islam	(Similar)	(Different) Buddhism

Cultural Patterns

(Different) Japan	(Similar)	(Different) Vietnam

Chinese Influences

(Different) Korea	(Similar)	(Different) Japan

Confucianism

(Different)	(Similar)	(Different)
Korea		China

The Americas

(Different)	(Similar)	(Different)
Maya		Inca

Europe

(Different)	(Similar)	(Different)
Feudalism		Cities

Christianity (Division)

(Different)	(Similar)	(Different)
Roman Catholic		Eastern Orthodox

Sudanic Empires

(Different) Songhay	(Similar)	(Different) Mali

South/Southeast Asia

(Different) Delhi Sultanate	(Similar)	(Different) Vietnam

Impact of Migrations

(Different) Afro-European	(Similar)	(Different) Americas

Impact of Plague Pandemics

(Different) Societal Consequences	(Similar)	(Different) Economic Consequences

Growth of Cities

(Different) China	(Similar)	(Different) Americas

Sources of Change

(Different) Nomadic Migrations	(Similar)	(Different) Urban Growth

Roles for Elite Women

(Different) Constraints	(Similar)	(Different) Opportunities

Dar al-Islam

(Different) Unified Political/Cultural Entity	(Similar)	(Different) Divided Political/Cultural Entity

Feudalism

(Different) Japanese	(Similar)	(Different) European

Development of Political/Social Institutions

(Different) Western Europe	(Similar)	(Different) Eastern Europe

Islamic Contacts

(Different) Sub-Saharan African	(Similar)	(Different) European

Political Entities

(Different) Arab Caliphate	(Similar)	(Different) Mamluks

European Feudalism

(Different) Serfs	(Similar)	(Different) Lords

Impact of the Crusades

(Different) Economic	(Similar)	(Different) Cultural

Impact of Viking Explorations

(Different) Economic	(Similar)	(Different) Cultural

Impact of Mongol Expansion

(Different) Economic	(Similar)	(Different) Cultural

Neo-Confucianism

(Different) Inside of China	(Similar)	(Different) Outside of China

Indian Ocean Trading Patterns

(Different) Hindu-Buddhist Period	(Similar)	(Different) Muslim Period

The Papacy

(Different) East–West Schism	(Similar)	(Different) Western Schism

Pre-Modern Era: 1450 to 1750

The Columbian Exchange

(Different)	(Similar)	(Different)
New World		**Old World**

Technological Changes

(Different)	(Similar)	(Different)
Shipbuilding		**Navigational Devices**

Major Empires

(Different)	(Similar)	(Different)
Ottoman		**China**

Major Empires

(Different)	(Similar)	(Different)
Mughal		**Tokugawa**

Major Empires

(Different) France	(Similar)	(Different) Russia

Major Empires

(Different) Portugal	(Similar)	(Different) Britain

Major Empires

(Different) Aztec	(Similar)	(Different) Spain

African Kingdoms

(Different) Kongo	(Similar)	(Different) Oyo

African Kingdoms

(Different)	(Similar)	(Different)
Benin		Dahomey

African Kingdoms

(Different)	(Similar)	(Different)
Ashanti		Songhay

Role of Women

(Different)	(Similar)	(Different)
In Households		In Politics

Slavery and the Slave Trade

(Different)	(Similar)	(Different)
Europe		Africa

Population Trends

(Different) North and South America	(Similar)	(Different) Europe and Africa

New Religions

(Different) Protestantism	(Similar)	(Different) Vodun

New Religions

(Different) Sikhism	(Similar)	(Different) Zen

Intellectual Developments

(Different) Scientific Revolution	(Similar)	(Different) Enlightenment

Developments in the Arts

(Different) Mughal	(Similar)	(Different) Europe

Developments in the Arts

(Different) East Asia	(Similar)	(Different) the Americas

Rising European Dominance

(Different) Environmental Reasons	(Similar)	(Different) Technological Reasons

Colonial Administrations

(Different) British	(Similar)	(Different) Spanish

Coercive Labor Systems

(Different) Indentured Service	(Similar)	(Different) Slavery

Development of Empires

(Different) Asia	(Similar)	(Different) Africa

Development of Empires

(Different) Americas	(Similar)	(Different) Europe

Imperial Systems

(Different) European Seaborne Empires	(Similar)	(Different) Asian Land-based Empires

Russia's Interactions with:

(Different) China	(Similar)	(Different) Ottoman Empire

Russia's Interactions with:

(Different) Western Europe	(Similar)	(Different) Eastern Europe

Economic Exchange Systems

(Different) Andean	(Similar)	(Different) Mesoamerican

Extent of Ottoman Expansion

(Different) Africa & Europe	(Similar)	(Different) Asia

Slave Plantation Systems

(Different) Old World	(Similar)	(Different) New World

Harems

(Different) Ottoman	(Similar)	(Different) Chinese

Trade Relationships

(Different) Kongo	(Similar)	(Different) Portugal

Foreign Policy (Relations)

(Different) Japan	(Similar)	(Different) Mughal

Foreign Policy (Relations)

(Different) European	(Similar)	(Different) Ottoman

European Exploration

(Different) Economic Reasons	(Similar)	(Different) Social/Cultural Reasons

European Absolutism

(Different) Political Consequences	(Similar)	(Different) Social Consequences

Protestant Reformation

(Different) Political Consequences	(Similar)	(Different) Social Consequences

Rise of the Modern Era: 1750 to 1914

Global Changes in:

(Different) Technology	(Similar)	(Different) Commerce

Global Changes in:

(Different) Communications	(Similar)	(Different) Trade Patterns

Global Changes in:

(Different) Demographic	(Similar)	(Different) Environmental

Global Changes in:

(Different) Medicines	(Similar)	(Different) Migration Patterns

Industrial Revolution

(Different) Europe	(Similar)	(Different) Americas

Industrial Revolution

(Different) Transformative Effects	(Similar)	(Different) Differential timing in opposing societies

Industrial Revolution

(Different) Social Impacts	(Similar)	(Different) Environmental Impacts

Emancipation

(Different) Slaves	(Similar)	(Different) Serfs

Societal Changes

(Different) Social Structures	(Similar)	(Different) Gender Roles/Structures

Political Movements & Independence Movements

(Different) United States	(Similar)	(Different) Latin America

Revolutions

(Different) France	(Similar)	(Different) China

Democracy Movements

(Different) Advances	(Similar)	(Different) Limitations

Rise of Western Dominance (Imperialism)

(Different) Military Aspects	(Similar)	(Different) Economic Aspects

Rise of Western Dominance (Imperialism)

(Different) Cultural Aspects	(Similar)	(Different) Political Aspects

Rise of Western Dominance (Imperialism)

(Different) Colonialism	(Similar)	(Different) Neocolonialism

Rise of Western Dominance (Imperialism)

(Different) Dissent & Reform	(Similar)	(Different) Resistance & Rebellion

European Art

(Different) African Influences	(Similar)	(Different) Asian Influences

Japan

(Different) Tokugawa	(Similar)	(Different) Meiji

Serf/Slave Emancipation

(Different) Causes	(Similar)	(Different) Effects

The Role of Women

(Different) Industrialized Regions	(Similar)	(Different) Non-Industrialized Regions

Technological Innovation

(Different)	(Similar)	(Different)
European/British		Asia/China

Latin American Independence Movements

(Different)	(Similar)	(Different)
Causes		Effects

Early Phase of the Industrial Revolution

(Different)	(Similar)	(Different)
Japan		Western European

Revolutions

(Different)	(Similar)	(Different)
American		French

Revolutions

(Different) Haitian	(Similar)	(Different) Mexican

Economic Systems & Theories

(Different) Capitalism	(Similar)	(Different) Marxism

Intellectual Developments

(Different) Darwinism	(Similar)	(Different) Social Darwinism

Reactions to Foreign Influence

(Different) Ottoman Empire	(Similar)	(Different) China

Reactions to Foreign Influence

(Different) India	(Similar)	(Different) Japan

Rise of Nationalism

(Different) Japan	(Similar)	(Different) China

Rise of Nationalism

(Different) Italy	(Similar)	(Different) Egypt

Rise of Nationalism

(Different) France	(Similar)	(Different) Germany

Rise of Nationalism

(Different) Pan Africanism	(Similar)	(Different) Indian Congress Movement

Forms of Western Intervention

(Different) East Asia	(Similar)	(Different) Southeast Asia

Forms of Western Intervention

(Different) Latin America	(Similar)	(Different) Africa

Conditions of Elite Women (before 1850)

(Different) Latin America	(Similar)	(Different) Western Europe

Contemporary Era: 1914 to Present

Women's Emancipation Movements

(Different) Europe	(Similar)	(Different) North America

Trade Networks

(Different) Suez Canal	(Similar)	(Different) Panama Canal

The World Wars

(Different) World War I	(Similar)	(Different) World War II

New Patterns of Nationalism

(Different) Fascism	(Similar)	(Different) Decolonization

Challenges to Democracy (Interwar Years)

(Different) Italy	(Similar)	(Different) Germany

Authoritarian Regimes (Interwar Years)

(Different) South America	(Similar)	(Different) Asia

War and Peace

(Different) The Holocaust	(Similar)	(Different) The Cold War

Global Political Structures

(Different)	(Similar)	(Different)
League of Nations		United Nations

Global Economic Structures

(Different)	(Similar)	(Different)
Developed Nations		Developing Nations

Decline of European Influence

(Different)	(Similar)	(Different)
United States		Asian Nations

War and Peace

(Different)	(Similar)	(Different)
Nuclear Weaponry		International Organizations

The Great Depression

(Different) The Americas	(Similar)	(Different) Europe

Social & Political Extremes

(Different) Racism (Apartheid)	(Similar)	(Different) Genocide

Global Economic Developments

(Different) Pacific Rim	(Similar)	(Different) Multinational Corporations

Social Changes

(Different) Changes in Gender Roles	(Similar)	(Different) Changes in Family Structures

Social Revolution

(Different) Peasant Revolutions	(Similar)	(Different) International Marxism

Social Reform

(Different) New Feminism	(Similar)	(Different) Religious Fundamentalism

Spread of Marxism/Communism

(Different) Russia	(Similar)	(Different) China

Soviet Union

(Different) Establishment	(Similar)	(Different) Disintegration

Post-Colonial Africa

(Different) Political Conflicts	(Similar)	(Different) Environmental Issues

Global Cultures

(Different) Science	(Similar)	(Different) Consumer Culture

Patterns of Resistance (Religious Responses)

(Different) South Asia	(Similar)	(Different) North America

Demographic Changes

(Different) Birth & Death Rates	(Similar)	(Different) Urban to Rural Shifts

Environmental Changes

(Different) Deforestation	(Similar)	(Different) Green/Environmental Movements

Diverse Interpretations

(Different) Cultural Diversity	(Similar)	(Different) Cultural Convergence

Frames of Reference

(Different) The West	(Similar)	(Different) The Developing World

Patterns of Decolonization

(Different) Africa	(Similar)	(Different) South Asia (India)

Effects on the Roles of Women

(Different) Iranian Revolution	(Similar)	(Different) Russian Revolution

Effects on the Roles of Women

(Different) Cuban Revolution	(Similar)	(Different) Chinese Revolution

Effects of the World Wars

(Different) In Africa	(Similar)	(Different) In Asia

Legacies of Colonialism

(Different) Middle East	(Similar)	(Different) Latin America

Legacies of Colonialism

(Different) Africa	(Similar)	(Different) Asia

Global Interactions

(Different) Sports	(Similar)	(Different) Arts

Effects of Western Consumer Society

(Different) Social/Cultural	(Similar)	(Different) Economic/Trade

Major Forms of 20th Century Warfare

(Different) The Great War	(Similar)	(Different) World War II

Major Forms of 20ᵗʰ Century Warfare

(Different) Terrorism	(Similar)	(Different) Guerilla

Cold War

(Different) Warsaw Pact	(Similar)	(Different) NATO

Effects of Global Wars

(Different) Economics	(Similar)	(Different) Political

Economic Growth in Asia

(Different) Japan	(Similar)	(Different) "The Little Tigers"

Creating Your Own Venn Diagrams Topic Charts:

The previous charts are far from complete and only provide a few examples of possible historical topics. A primary objective of this activity is to activate a student's prior knowledge, while simultaneously connecting this existing knowledge to the newly learned information. Once educators are familiar with the format, strategy, and information in the charts; they should expand the amount of material used in this activity and create their own diagrams. The main point to remember is that the terms or ideas need to possess elements that are related in both a similar and dissimilar way. The ability to compare and contrast large amounts of information is at the very core of critical thinking, and possessing this capacity is what allows students to generate thoughtful inferences and evaluations.

(Different)	(Similar)	(Different)

(Different)	(Similar)	(Different)

(Different)	(Similar)	(Different)
_____		_____

(Different)	(Similar)	(Different)
_____		_____

(Different)	(Similar)	(Different)
_____		_____

For more information about the *Teaching for Recall & Analysis* series of books visit:

www.teachingforrecall.com

www.ingramcontent.com/pod-product-compliance
Lightning Source LLC
Chambersburg PA
CBHW080534090426
42733CB00015B/2581